PREHISTORIC
ACTUAL
SIZE

"Morgan's tooth"
200 million years ago
4-inch-long (10-centimeter-long) body

BY STEVE JENKINS

HOUGHTON MIFFLIN HARCOURT
BOSTON NEW YORK

Velociraptor (vee-*lohs*-i-*rap*-tor) was a swift, agile predator that may have been covered with feathers.

75 million years ago
6 ½ feet (2 meters) long

Animals have lived on earth for hundreds of millions of years. Dragonflies the size of seagulls, meat-eating dinosaurs bigger than a bus, giant flying reptiles, fierce predatory birds eight feet tall — they all appeared, thrived for millions of years, and then died out as the world changed around them. In this book you'll see what these pre-historic animals, along with many others, may have looked like at **actual size.**

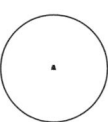

One of the first animals to appear on Earth was a tiny, hard-shelled **protozoan** (pro-toh-*zoh*-an). It was almost too small to see.

550 million years ago
¹⁄₂₅ inch (1 millimeter) across

The sharp-eyed **sea scorpion** hunted in shallow seas.

420 million years ago
6 ½ feet (2 meters) long

The tiny **spiny shark,** one of the first
fishes, was protected by armor plates
and sharp spines.

410 million years ago
3 inches (8 centimeters) long

Diplocaulus (*dip*-lo-*cawl*-lus) was a meat-eating amphibian. Its horns may have helped it glide through the water.

300 million years ago
3 feet (91 centimeters) long

Imagine a **dragonfly** with wings more than two feet across!

300 million years ago
27-inch (69-centimeter) wingspan

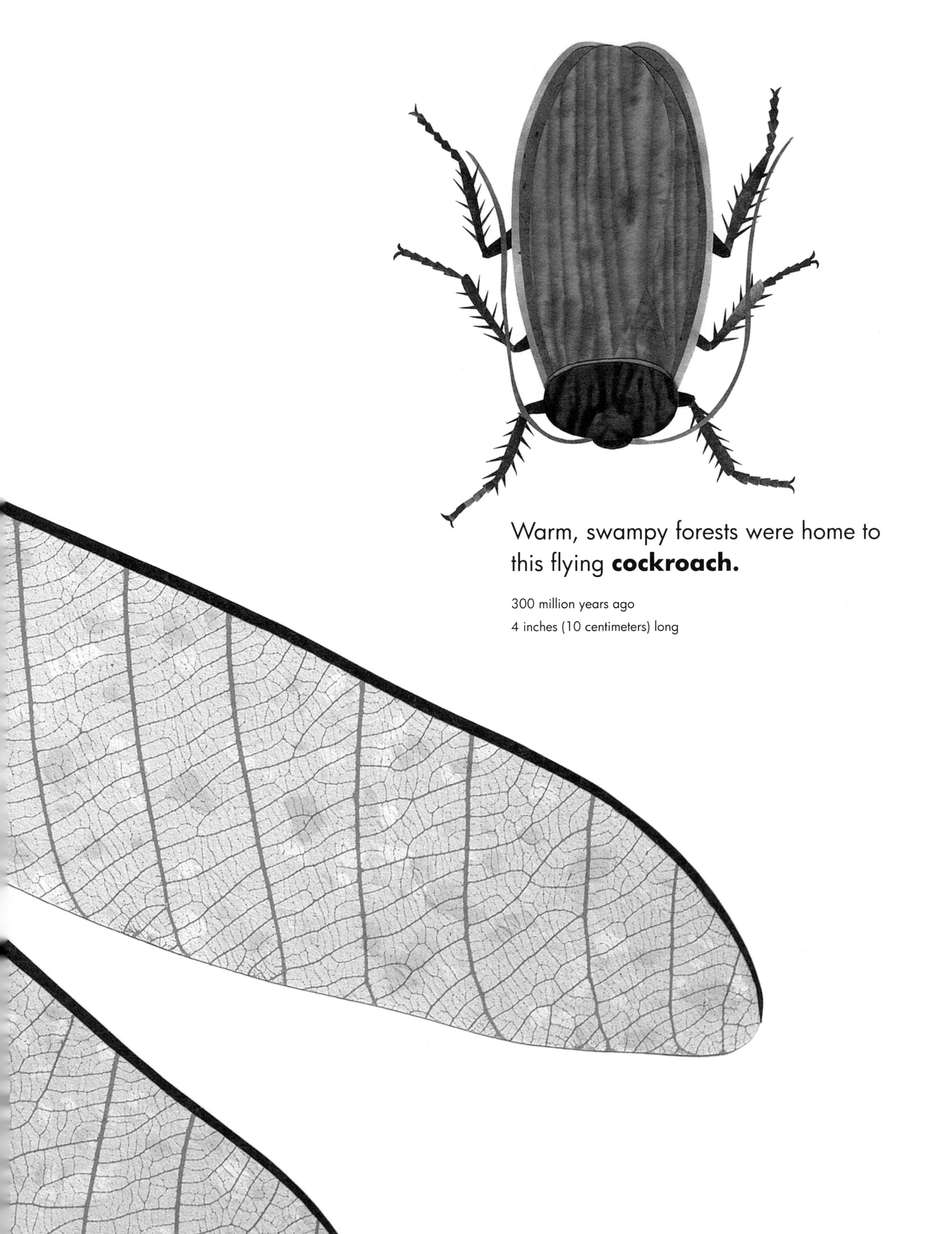

Warm, swampy forests were home to this flying **cockroach.**

300 million years ago
4 inches (10 centimeters) long

This giant **millipede** had as many as thirty pairs of legs.

300 million years ago
6 ½ feet (2 meters) long

Despite its name, **Dinocephalosaurus** (*di*-no-*sef*-ah-lo-*sawr*-us) wasn't a dinosaur. It was a fish-eating reptile that sucked up its prey by quickly stretching out its long neck.

230 million years ago
8 feet (2½ meters) long

The bird-like **Saltopus** (*salt*-oh-pus), one of the smallest dinosaurs, was a swift runner.

210 million years ago
2 feet (61 centimeters) long

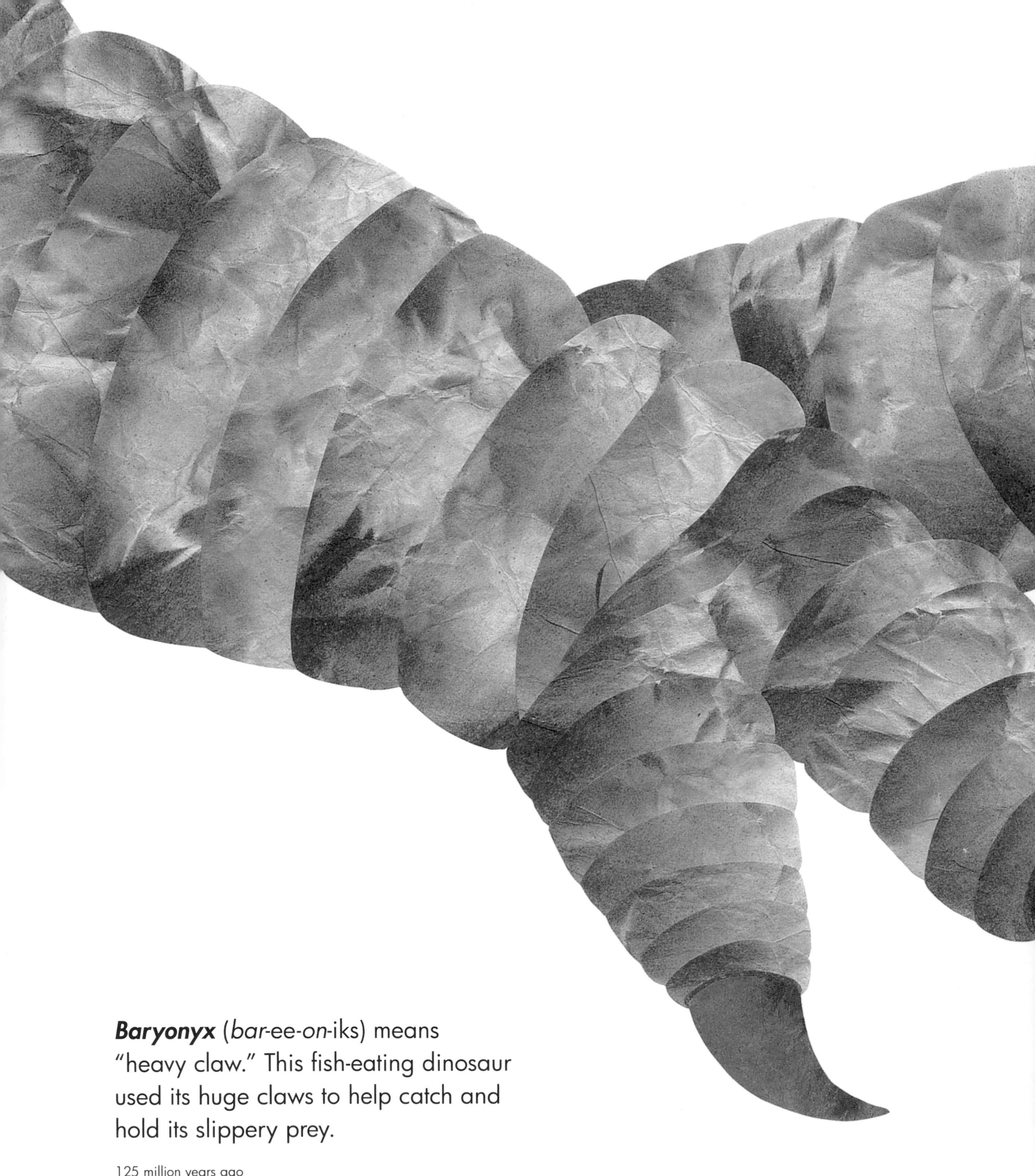

Baryonyx (*bar-ee-on-*iks) means "heavy claw." This fish-eating dinosaur used its huge claws to help catch and hold its slippery prey.

125 million years ago
33 feet (10 meters) long

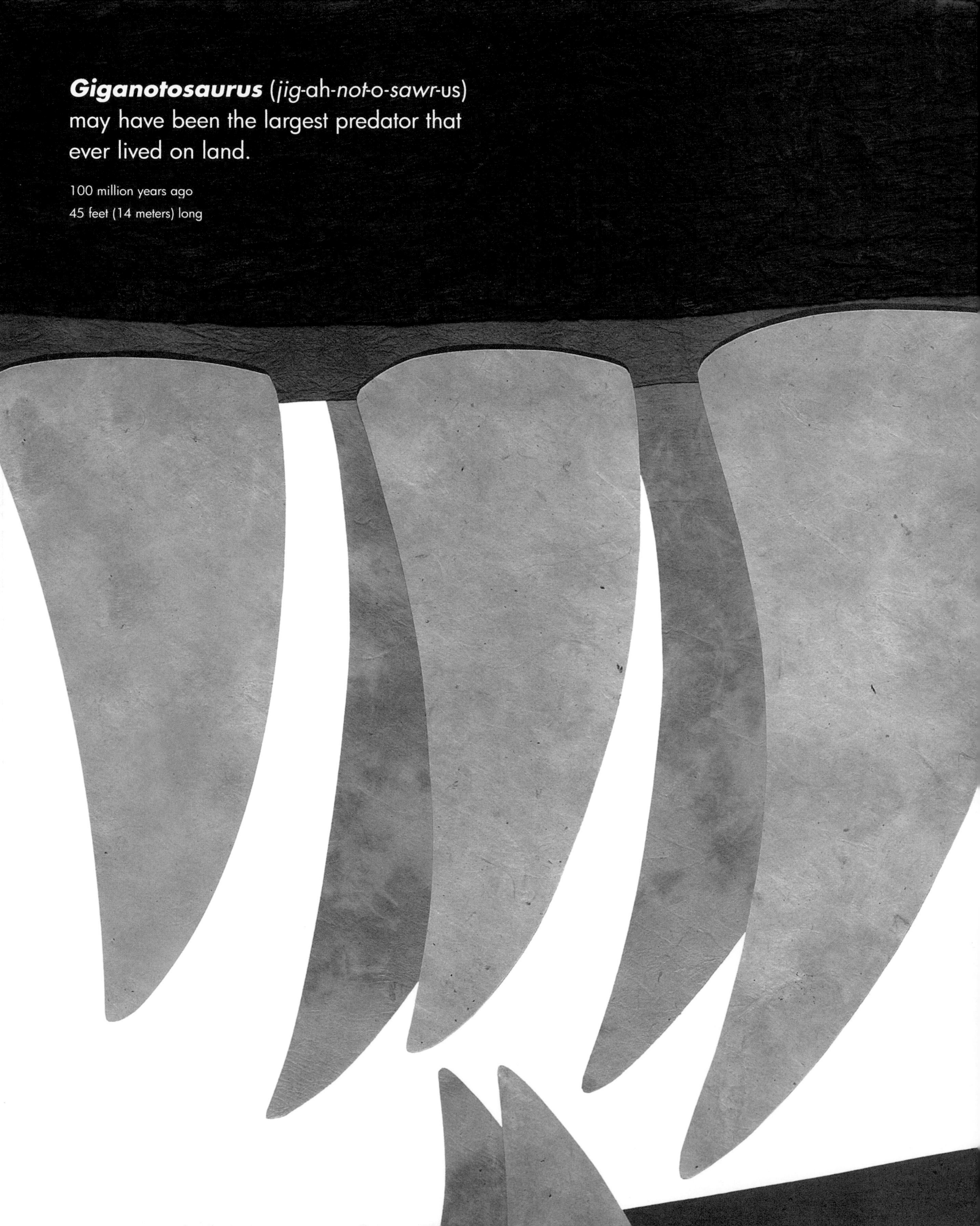

Giganotosaurus (*jig-ah-not-o-sawr-*us) may have been the largest predator that ever lived on land.

100 million years ago

45 feet (14 meters) long

Protoceratops (*pro*-toh-*ser*-a-tops) was a plant-eating dinosaur that used its sharp beak to bite through tough stems and leaves. A baby *Protoceratops* was only about six inches (15 centimeters) long when it hatched.

80 million years ago
6 feet (183 centimeters) long

Leptictidium (*lep*-tik-*tid*-ee-um), an insect-eating mammal, hopped about on its back legs.

45 million years ago
2 feet (61 centimeters) long

The **terror bird** lived in South America.
It was the largest predator of its time
— big enough to eat a horse.

3 million years ago
8 feet (2½ meters) tall

How do we know what prehistoric animals looked like? Fossils, which preserve the form of ancient bones and teeth, can tell us a lot about animals that lived a long time ago. By comparing these fossils to the skeletons of animals that are alive today, we can get a good idea of an animal's size and shape, how it moved, and what kinds of food it ate. In a few rare fossils, the imprint of skin, scales, or feathers is preserved. Fossils, however, can't tell us what color an animal was or whether it had spots, stripes, or other patterns. A small plant-eating animal that lived among the trees, like a present-day deer, was probably a dull color to help it blend in with its environment. A hunting animal that lived on the open plains may have been the color of dry grass, like a modern-day African lion. A predator that stalked its prey in the forest could have had stripes like a tiger that helped camouflage it. Other animals may have attracted mates or signaled others of their kind with patches of bright color, like many modern birds and lizards. The patterns and colors of the animals in this book are best guesses based on how ancient animals lived and on the appearance of modern animals that live the same way.

Morganucodon (*mor*-gan-*u*-co-don), which means "Morgan's tooth," was a primitive mammal that lived 200 million years ago. It was small, with a body only about four inches (ten centimeters) long. Its large eyes suggest that it was active at night, which would have helped it hide from the many predatory reptiles and dinosaurs that lived at the same time. "Morgan's tooth" probably had a keen sense of smell, and it fed on insects and worms.

Velociraptor (vee-*lohs*-i-*rap*-tor) was a quick and aggressive predatory dinosaur that lived about 75 million years ago. It had sharp fangs and claws, with a special "killing claw" several inches long on each back foot. It was a fast runner that probably hunted in

packs. Though small for a dinosaur — only about six and a half feet (two meters) long and weighing around 30 pounds (14 kilograms) — several *Velociraptors* working together could bring down prey much larger than themselves. Recently, many scientists who study dinosaurs have suggested that *Velociraptor* and other birdlike dinosaurs were covered with feathers, probably to help them keep warm.

Single-celled **protozoa** (pro-toh-*zoh*-a) were among the first organisms to appear on earth. These simple creatures had ornate shells in the shape of spirals, stars, or cones. Though they were very small — many of their fossils are barely visible to the naked eye — their shells accumulated on the ocean floor in unimaginable numbers, where time and pressure gradually turned them into limestone. In some parts of the world, as mountains were formed and continents shifted, the ocean floor was lifted high above the water. In these places the fossilized skeletons of these tiny creatures can be seen today as limestone cliffs thousands of feet tall.

The **sea scorpion** was one of the top predators of its time. It hunted fish and other small animals in warm, shallow seas some 420 million years ago. This ancestor of the lobster grew to be six and a half feet (two meters) long. It had good eyesight and large clawlike fangs. Some sea scorpions were able to breathe air and could climb onto the land.

Many early fish, such as the **spiny shark,** were heavily armored to protect them from larger predators. This small meat eater, about the size of a pet goldfish, appeared about 410 million years ago. Armored fish, some the size of a bus, would swim in the earth's seas, rivers, and lakes for the next 170 million years.

Three hundred million years ago the dominant animals on earth were amphibians, the ancestors of today's frogs and salamanders. Some of these animals were sharp-toothed hunters over ten feet (three meters) long. Others looked like eels or snakes. One of the oddest

was **Diplocaulus** (*dip*-lo-*cawl*-us), an aquatic animal three feet (91 centimeters) long. It had large winglike horns that might have acted as fins, helping the animal glide through the water. These horns might also have helped protect *Diplocaulus* from predators by making it hard to swallow.

The largest insect that ever lived was an ancient relative of the **dragonfly.** It hunted some 300 million years ago in the forests of what is now Europe. With wings 27 inches (69 centimeters) across, it was a frightening aerial predator. Like a modern dragonfly, it was a speedy flier that could change direction quickly, grabbing smaller insects out of the air and eating them on the fly.

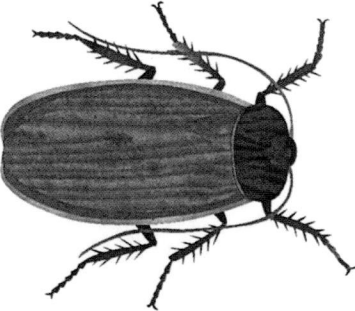

The **cockroach** is one of the oldest living animals. Cockroaches of one kind or another have been around for more than 300 million years. Some of these early cockroaches were huge — up to four inches (10 centimeters) long. They lived in warm, swampy fern forests.

Arthropods are animals with hard-shelled, jointed bodies, such as insects, crabs, scorpions, and centipedes. They are a very ancient group of animals that first appeared more than 500 million years ago. The largest arthropod ever to live on land was a giant **millipede** that lived about 300 million years ago. It grew to six and a half feet (two meters) long, and probably burrowed into the forest floor, feeding on decaying plant material.

Dinocephalosaurus (*di-no-sef-ah-lo-sawr-us*), which means "terrible-headed lizard," hunted fish in warm, shallow seas about 230 million years ago. Its neck was more than twice as long as its body. Overall, it was about eight feet (two and a half meters) in length. This reptile's head, perched at the end of its long neck, would have looked like just another small fish as it approached its prey in murky water. When it was close enough, *Dinocephalosaurus* was able to quickly expand its throat and suck up its unlucky victim.

Not all dinosaurs were big. **Saltopus** (*salt-oh-pus*) was a birdlike animal that ran on two long legs. It weighed about two pounds (one kilogram) — the same as a large squirrel. *Saltopus* lived 210 million

years ago, and was one of the first dinosaurs to appear. It used its speed and needle-sharp teeth to catch and eat insects and other small animals.

Flying reptiles, or pterosaurs (*ter-o-sawrs*), first appeared about 215 million years ago. As a group, they survived for the next 150 million years. Some were the size of a small bird. Others were gigantic, with wings 36 feet (11 meters) across. **Dsungaripterus** (*jung-ah-rip-ter-us*) was a medium-sized pterosaur, with leathery wings ten feet (three meters) wide, that lived about 135 million years ago. Its fossils are often found on the shores of what were once lakes and seas, where these flying predators may have nested and raised their young in colonies. *Dsungaripterus* had a curved beak with strong, blunt teeth, probably used for catching, prying open, and crushing crabs and shellfish. The crest on this reptile's head may have been used to signal a mate. Perhaps the crest was brightly colored, like the mating displays of many present-day reptiles and birds.

Baryonyx (*bar-ee-on-iks*) was one of the only dinosaurs known to eat fish. This two-ton (1,800-kilogram) predator lived about 125 million years ago. Compared to other large predatory dinosaurs that walked on their back legs, *Baryonyx* was unusual. It had long jaws, like a crocodile's. Instead of tiny front arms, *Baryonyx* had large arms with huge, sharp thumb claws that helped it grasp its slippery prey. All of these adaptations made *Baryonyx* very effective at catching fish.

Giganotosaurus (*jig*-ah-*not*-o-*sawr*-us), perhaps the largest land predator that has ever lived, stalked the plains of South America 100 million years ago. This dinosaur looked like a bigger, heavier version of the more familiar *Tyrannosaurus rex*. It was 45 feet (14 meters) long and may have weighed as much as eight tons (7,250 kilograms). At this size, it could attack even huge 100-ton (91,000-kilogram) plant-eating dinosaurs.

Protoceratops (*pro*-toh-*ser*-a-tops) was a plant eater with a big head, a sharp beak, and a bony frill around its neck. We don't know if *Protoceratops* took care of its babies when they hatched or if they were left to fend for themselves. Though it wasn't a large dinosaur, *Protoceratops* could defend itself with its armor and its pointed beak. It was about six feet (183 centimeters) long and lived around 80 million years ago.

Leptictidium (*lep*-tik-*tid*-ee-um) made its home on the forest floor about 45 million years ago, where it ate insects and other small animals. There were several different species of these mammals. The one in this book was about two feet (61 centimeters) long and could move quickly, hopping on its big back legs. *Leptictidium* had a long, flexible nose that it used to sniff out food.

For millions of years the top predators in South America were large, flightless birds. One of these fierce hunters was known as the **terror bird**. It lived until about three million years ago. The largest of the terror birds stood eight feet (two and a half meters) tall. It had strong feet and claws and a huge, sharp beak, and probably could run as fast as a present-day horse.

Rodents first appeared more than 50 million years ago. **Epigaulus** (ep-ee-*gaw*-lus), a North American burrowing rodent, had long claws for digging and two horns that may have been used for self-defense. *Epigaulus* was about the size of a rabbit and lived some five million years ago. A South American relative of *Epigaulus,* an enormous guinea pig the size of a rhinoceros, was the largest rodent that has ever lived.

For Robin

The text of this book is set in Futura.
The illustrations are collages of cut and torn paper.

The Library of Congress has cataloged the hardcover edition as follows:
Jenkins, Steve, 1952–
Prehistoric actual size / by Steve Jenkins.
p. cm.
1. Dinosaurs—Size—Juvenile literature. I. Title.
QE861.5 J46 2005
560—dc22
2004025124

ISBN: 978-0-618-53578-1 hardcover
ISBN: 978-0-544-58238-5 paperback

Manufactured in Malaysia
TWP 10 9 8 7
4500769976

Epigaulus (ep-ee-*gaw*-lus) was a rodent that lived underground. It had long claws and horns on its head.

5 million years ago
12 inches (30 centimeters) long